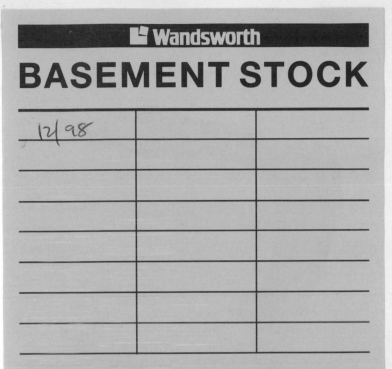

Peter Ackroyd was born in London in 1949. He is a graduate of Cambridge University and was a Mellon Fellow at Yale. He has been literary editor of *The Spectator* and is now chief book reviewer for *The Times*.

Peter Ackroyd's biography, *T. S. Eliot*, was awarded the Whitbread Prize for the best biography published in 1984, and was joint winner of the Royal Society of Literature's William Heinemann Award. His novel, *The Last Testament of Oscar Wilde*, won the Somerset Maugham Award and his most recent work of fiction, *Hawksmoor*, has been awarded both the Guardian Fiction Award and the Whitbread Prize for the best novel published in 1985.

PETER ACKROYD

The Diversions of Purley

and other poems

ABACUS

100.867696

AN ABACUS BOOK

First published in Great Britain
by Hamish Hamilton Ltd 1987
Published by Sphere Books Ltd in Abacus 1990

ISBN 0 3491 0131 0

Printed and bound in Great Britain by
Richard Clay Ltd, Bungay, Suffolk

Sphere Books Ltd
A Division of
Macdonald & Co. (Publishers) Ltd
Orbit House, 1 New Fetter Lane, London EC4A 1AR
A member of Maxwell Macmillan Pergamon Publishing Corporation

For Kevin Stratford

The streets of a great city when they are empty. I have a pain in my finger although everything is happening at once although it cannot be seen. The light is making a vague noise and so I move closer to myself. The sign ahead of me says, 'Have another before you' and then I see a small figure dart behind the hoarding. The colours of the advertisement get brighter as the sun rises above the buildings and I know the noise will increase. My finger still hurts but I will soon be in a place of unimaginable pleasure. But also it is just an ordinary day.

According to the patient, he woke up shortly afterwards, feeling very thirsty. It is probable that at the moment the dream vanished the subject was about to walk into the red building opposite. The dream therefore satisfies a need to enter the building, or perhaps the colour red.

Besides, the dream most often fulfils a cascade of older and older wishes: the smell of his own hand, the translation of a foreign poem, or the great city itself.

What indifferent elements of the previous day are to be found in the manifest text of the dream in our example? Jeremy had written *to his father* about the frequency of *the buses*. They had met for the first time and had noticed *the truces* in each other's *faces*, indicating one of the places where the pleasure came to rest. The father said, *'It's been a long time since I walked here.'*

The analytic technique of free association around the manifest elements also allows three childhood memories to come to light:

(i)   the pain in the great city, where the sun is a noise.

(ii)   a walk in unimaginable pleasure, which is covered with *faces*.

(iii)   an advertisement which conceals the fleeing figure.

Analysis of the dream takes us back, then, to the fundamental declaration, 'Have another before you', addressed to Jeremy (Jay-ray-mee). Over and above the real satisfaction of the red building, the dream refers back to an unconscious wish to go, to an oral instinct directed towards the sun.

The instinct introduces an erotic quality into the sphere of need. The instinct as such has no place in the psychical apparatus and only enters into it through the mediation of *Spaltung*. It is the voice in the room next to mine.

And everyone heard the wrong story
                my terrific love-cries
                are probably for sale
the technician said, "these poems are a wounded
                        fawn":
oh the strange story of the quantum!
                if I smile will she smile
                no one smiles, your eyes
                are like broken glass are
                you unemployed?

What do these words mean? (a) love-cries
(b) quantum (c) unemployed.
Have you ever met anyone with eyes
like broken glass? If you have, write about it.
If not, would you like to? Why?
Read the poem again, and think about
the last lines. Why was nobody smiling?
Try to explain in your own words how
the writer felt when he saw the girl
with eyes like broken glass.

Your writing is peaceful now, and so starve
    Your dream which looked at itself and drowns
When Mr Harding reached the parsonage he
    Found that the arch-deacon had been called away
And a natural hush falls over us, all in your
    Arms. The flowers fold over the grass
And respire, there are no persons in the walk,
    For all this is seen through the window.
Why should I enter only to fall on my arse ah
    Ah the pity of it all trickles like purity
That the babba might lisp its fair syllable
    And sip the proffered cup.

This is a giant Race before the Flood flying
    Before you "how can we pretend to describe
The rapture with which Mr Harding was received"
    Let small stones be our path until we fall
Asleep and then speak willingly, wet your hair
    Apply, lather, rinse and oh repeat that
Repeat until the billion names of God
    Put out the firmament and the stones cry
Ma Ba Ta. The sermon is now complete it is a
    Vague hush as your mechanical song
Fills the garden, and the leaves turn red
    And then black.

and the children . . .

i

and the children who see everything
forget : what is separate
is also in succession, the will empties
and is replaced by the shape
of moving things

as you were running beside me
and night comes on,
a room is a fragile place
in which to remember
and catch the warmth as it flies

second by second
to recreate what was not created,
making the figure still
as it was at first sight,
the half-light upon the floor

it would be easy to get lost
in a prosaic description of this light
on water, clause upon clause
opening out into a definition of light
praised for its subtlety and distance

talking in your sleep
is another way, the evidence of senses
left in bewilderment
at the sight of all there is
the soul creeping into the dark

each thing with its own wish to grow
and avert its face,
the penniless young man
smiles at the light
the nearest thing to oblivion

This beautiful fruit . . .

This beautiful fruit broken off the tree
a veiled remembrance of all this reality . . .
so now I go sailing into the empyrean
where my poems may glitter like cars :
we will not see each other, the girl said,
and we will be happy. Night, with its promise
of night, will not return. The perfect stranger
has sailed with me, like a phantom limb.
"Just look up at the stars! The stars!"

Yes, they are dead. The face you don't see
is your own, you see only the light
coiling through childish groves and swamps.
What is it that makes these things exist?
I woke up, and her words were like trees
around me. We said things, and lived
in order to live, while giants were huffing
and puffing somewhere; we do not grow wise,
we are lying down without rhyme or reason.

There are so many . . .

'There are so many useless things to be done
and, conversely, there are external forces
which can no longer be organised or controlled.'
Think of all the leaves on a single tree
and the way that winter pulls them down
until nothing in the wood will grow.
Connections must now be made with human love,
as if it were a story in which the ending
has never been understood. I am going on with it
just to see what happens.

On page one the children stretch their limbs
and then on page four they run into the forest
where giants part the leaves and peer at them.
On page thirteen the darkness grows like a tree,
and this is the part that no one understands.
It might be better to begin at the beginning
and read the story for examples of bad grammar,
sloppy characterisation, literals and so forth . . .
'At night I like to look up at the stars
and when I wake up I am glad to be alone,
just as things are brightest when they are stopped
in mid-career.'

my own and not my own
   each thing grows or grows
and I fall into a swoon

   the heat is upon me
like a voice as the voice
   recedes into a point

X marks the spot
   where all my fears begin
turning like dancers

   sleep glows in their arms
while the bright medal is worn
   warding off sickness

as I walk and walk
   pinpoints of light reflect
the dry, enormous plain.

the stone . . .

I

        the stone has turned its face away beginning
with its clarity
                the minute we escaped we see
        the watcher and the watched

       "he's drunk he is asleep in the garden"

           to touch the other side and the seasons
     hide themselves

     arranged in their order of brightness

II

the engraving of Corvus Corax or the common raven is above
the desk where he works by night and by day

           that the paper bag
    casts its shadow whose intimate edges

  the old gang bicycling side by side

              you were wearing
   a blue shirt and blue pants

  you said, riddle me a riddle!

III

everyone began
to make copies of themselves

in the twi twi twilight

the glass was not disturbed it was
perfectly posed

did you hear about the lives
of the others how their words were drowned

just a slice of blue showing

IV

that were all caught in expression of disbelief and horror,
going about their daily tasks

the beaded bubbles winking
at the brim

hey, the progress of human societies
into a sexual maelstrom . . .

"We are against it!
it will never happen!"

it is . . .

it is the subject which speaks
these leaves are a signal
of one colour upon another
as broad as the rise of fascism

into a closed form of verse
the marble child rests
in the arms of his message
tracing letters in the air

I cannot see the others
because I am there
where the shoe speaks
and the statue moves

this sequence of feelings
is described in the head
as a hymn to feeling
leading me forward

into the wooden O
o the body falls behind
its words, which exist
in this place and are calm

a dialogue

He said, the day is like a code
No, she said, it is clearly over

As a reflection upon glass I
But a solid object cannot last

dream of things I do not see
What of the world which needs

Here is where I sleep and sleep
the sensation of being seized

until I can reach no further
And whom will you have left behind

one picture becomes the same picture
She is alone and stays alone

the image being of an image
like an image of what you say

the rooks (after Andrew Lanyon)

everything is clearer before you jump
        into the ideal order
    in which you are diminished
            and from all this activity comes silence
        as Mr. Lewis Harding observes the rooks
through the wrong end of his telescope :

10th December, 1847
'5.00 p.m. Dark and no rooks arrived! - First time since this
journal began that the rooks have failed to return. They have
always returned at least an hour before dark, today I know not
what has become of them, they have not been seen in the
neighbourhood . . .'

        and so·they turned and rose
        like small verbs making their line immortal

all we have knowledge of is our own time
        the shape in the water is your own
    the pattern of fixed moments
            falling away as you watch

we must wait for the collapse
        before we can start a new life
    indistinct now as the sky fills with wings

Only connect . . .

i

      Only connect
sounds of love
              come from the head
   in a fixed handwriting
                    name following name
    the heart
         is beating like a sign
     of love as dog chases duck
among natural signs :

       sketching the especial scene
by numbers,
         14 is the heart
   9 is the name
       which has been erased
I wrote his word
           upon the sand
   and I felt nothing.

ii

The minor characters wither in the light which I have
        created
out of hoots and puffs, Captain Scarlet and poor dear Joe
        are lost
among a stream of tiny objects which fall and gash
        vermillion,
look down and see your own face blurred among all this
        suffering
as if you were changed by it.

My favourite poem is from 1638
look down and read the fine print
filling my mind with lost objects
so calm so bright they help me sleep

on waking up and looking at the day
like an engraving in a penny dreadful
look down and read the faces of the crowd
silent as if seen through a window

knocking in vain, their words like gas,
something has died in tremendous suffering.
Could I lay my hand on it, as in amusement,
as you watch a small boat from a bridge?

iv.

The same words have come out of the dark as you will know it
like a secret ray holding your face in a fixed position
as the time lag increases,
clap your hands if you believe in Tinker Bell
coming out of the dark
with a song which makes no noise.

v.

'The days are over now but they still hold
our gaze wasting our lives in their light
the eye moves in its case from left to right
as the lights grow smaller and smaller
(but we may die in their heat!)
until they appear in a fixed pattern
and the days are left in silence like rooms.'

vi.

The consumers in the great urban centre
heard this song and were moved by it,
it rose in a straight line with a tiny light
seen in the mind's eye as a phoneme.
It was an idea which had not been discovered
and their voices changed on the soft notes
making their faces all alike in factories,
offices and homes. Outside,
a child pretends he is a plane and spreads
his arms.

the cut in . . .

                    the cut in my sleep
              an adventure in slow rhyme
                          begins in the forehead

              its image of hurt
                 conceals the light it brings
        you will not know one another

                          noises in the dark
                  are a continuation
                          leading into the dark

           which bears everything
                      just as the blindness
              bringing us forward

      in perpetual motion
                 pushing all of the buttons
                          in the new hotel

           standing in the wind
   against the wind
              making it plausible

           because of the cold
        and then, seeing you,
                 I am a rhyme for 'weep'

the novel

So this is the way it should be,
with everything there just to be described
like landscapes, seascapes or family portraits
which seem most real when they are not so.
If only it could always be like this
and then I might hit upon some true feelings :
outside the girls are singing 'Ragtime'
and then of course I start singing it too.
Ah these people, I wish I could immortalise them
like Ronald Firbank or even Graham Greene . . . well,
they are wearing sweaters saying 'Crisis? What Crisis?',
their breath can be traced like pale branches,
here today and gone tomorrow OK?

So winter is coming in, and the self fades
and flickers; we read novels late into the night,
watching helplessly as characters race toward each other
until the screams and whistles finally die down
and a faint violet spreads across the margin.
So much has been written about this light, both for
and against, I don't know how to begin —
where the stars go? how the day starts?
Angel Clare bows his head against the wind,
thinking about the things he has to do today :
if I come out into the open will I be myself,
or will it be the beginning of another story?

the poem

so   the way
                        to be described
      landscapes   or   portraits
which seem
   only
                                    true feelings
              are singing
                        singing it
            I wish I
                                                well,
they are
                  traced
      today and gone

                              self fades
                        into
                                          each other
            and   finally
               spreads across
      has been written
         I don't know how to
               how
                        against the wind
thinking about
                              will I be
            the beginning

In the middle . . .

In the middle of nowhere
you adopt this uncertain expression

as though you had lived for 'significant form'
and then forgot your own name

first the orange, then the red, then the rest,
these unpleasant sensations

which becomes strobe lighting :
tiredness, anxiety, the willingness to please,

impatience and finally anger.
Ten forties minus three sixteens equals

the answer you need.
Speak to me now in your certainty.

there was no rain . . .

There was no rain all that summer
and life decreased. Why do one thing or the other?
The clouds spun in heavenly harmony
but to no earthly purpose.
It was time to write that poem
about the way the broad leaves look for water
until their stalks fall down upon the ground . . .

the afternoon woke up with a shout
and then it was gone, leaving a clear light
which has lasted day in and day out.
When I think of it I get this sicky feeling,
this light might go on for ever
and then my personality would never change!
The trees knelt and still the rain held off.

the day . . .

the day has been drawn off
into a shoulder of brown cloth

the vehicle waits
in which she sits, unencumbered

the child already
marked in that way

the pain comes in
the song of the tin man

and the song has gone
I think this is what Eliot meant
except that I don't think

the words are short
in the mouth, tranquility
is not one of them

Lovers But Still Strangers

I kept thinking the whole thing wasn't real. It was like something out of a movie. Feeling ashen inside, I went back into the apartment to face my past. Had God given up on me? Garth called it love, but I called it rape. I should have realised before what it was, and that he used me and our baby, but when you love, you can be blind. I felt a sudden tightness in my throat, a deep-down ache that seemed to spread through my whole body. Then it seemed I heard my own voice coming from far away. "Maybe it would be better if we didn't see each other any more." Garth's lean, handsome face was dark with anger. His eyes glittered like black agate. He did not know that everything I said was for his own sake. I felt tears wet my lashes. I was older and sadder somehow, and a little wistful. You could have stirred my knees with a spoon. "Please Lita," he begged, "you're driving me crazy. You know I love you."

That was three months ago. Since then I've been seeing Monty every day and he's already begun to talk about marriage. Perhaps, in the end, only God can make the final judgement. I hope He judges me kindly. And somehow, someday, when enough time has gone by, maybe I will too.

Continued on page 50

how did it . . .

    how did it grow up?
    like a stick

        it was left in the dark
           filled and emptied

where is the connection
  between one and another?

             which doesn't break
                as it sinks

        a world with a mild buzz
      stretch out the hand slowly

    reaching nothing
    it stays the same

             where he walks unaccompanied
               this pale blue light

      what has happened to him
      is a balloon

a face painted on it
  it is invisible

            he might reach it
            he hopes

    and then become the meaning
      of what he will become

on the third . . .

on the third stroke
it will be uncertain

my dreams meet me half-way
stunned and incomplete

you repeated something
and then I walked forward

the lines meet in the distance
touching someone's life

there is a place I cannot reach
where the others are

this is my life here,
like a stretch of water

the poem is made of sleep
speech slowed down to the nth degree

the storm in my head
will not reach its point

out of the . . .

i

out of the corner of your eye
the darkness starts crowding in
limitless, undisciplined like a shout
repeated over and over
until the throat becomes dry

what is the expression for it,
when the night stares you in the face
and then turns away?
Is it, goodnight Eileen
nice seeing you?

ii

as the light steps backward
becoming grey
what is the subject?
a splash somewhere
but the artist keeps still

hoping to change the change
into an idea
where no one is present
although in the same room
the artist broke his thumb

iii.

at night I lift down
large blocks of stone
ready for stacking

the heat of the race
leaves the sweat empty
which is not so dark

here it is surrounded
by the face of things
which is asleep

within us
the understanding between
has no depth

the dark hand touches
the light hand
in the same field

white, light blue and grey
with the signs for
orange and aquamarine

rising with it
like Star Wars music
into a future problem

the day is its halo
sometimes freedom
and sometimes it is not

the inner light
is also a sign
of peace among men

in the middle of stones
which beckon to you
like a child's drawing

life isn't a gamble
life isn't tragedy
life isn't really anything

The extreme heat . . .

The extreme heat of endless days
touching in their majesty and a sign
of human progress : the pollen count
keeps abreast of our enormous worries.

But the purlieus rivet our gaze,
an inkling of woods and streams will last
into galleries : its gigantic light
spreads decision into homes of crime.

Vast drinking fountains merge into
indifference, heat briefs the vistas
for new kinds of response: the faces
we knew are helpless and do not exist.

How did it all begin? It was a boy
and his terrific indolence . . . the audience
sighs bitterly: 'Did you keep the
repellent cream? Where are the tickets?'

madness . . .

madness on the vines
the dusty light
in which I lose myself

a refreshing ice-cream
is dipped into the sea
of brilliant lights

leaving these fears behind
in a flat landscape
where nothing moves

the light is dipped
into a refreshing madness
where nothing moves

brilliant, I lose
this dusty landscape
behind myself

I am anxious about my work,
my job, my social life,
my future and the present

just think,
I carry ice-cream around
the whole day

Across the street . . .

Across the street Fun City was opening up. It was one of those days. Joe sat on the edge of his bed, a photograph. Poor naked Bedlam. Joe's a'cold. The rain fell in towels. Nobody believes in anything any more, sang the thrush, and the dawn fell quiet. But I believe in Joe. He rose to brush his teeth, it was the early afternoon. Now comes the time for avoidance. The passers-by hardly notice his fixed smile as he walks to Fun City, he is smiling because he is the proprietor. "Nice sleep, Joe?". The pinball machines are inhuman really, but their lights are so pretty : people spend all day in here sometimes, using their salaries. The full throated note of the swan is not heard. Reflections like these dampen Joe's good spirits, but he keeps on smiling. That is why Fun City is so successful. Night falls.

the room is . . .

the room is full of turbulent signs
but the new facts are avoided
I wake up as a different person :
the body rests upon light covers
the covers are lit by the body
the body is covered with light
light covers the body
and the body itself is weightless

a burnt match becomes a flame
your identity ceases to matter
the moment before this moment
when the mirror becomes an explosion
hey buddy can you spare a dime
I've never laughed so long or loud
at the figure in the red and green
whose body itself is weightless

waiting for sounds that do not come
though the smoke itself gathers
and the rest refuses to be known
out of the chaos emerges a child
who will walk as if in a trance
and the flame is a slow thing
it will hide the quick landscape
he knows his body is weightless

because it cannot be known there
where the words are sufficient
to forget the noise of his words
this is the new age
where the narrator knows everything
so everything is at peace
the flame is a figure of eight
and the figure is weightless

you see into your own face
but the features are not your own
they are a vague photograph
of a moving light on a body
which will not rest in the light
as long as the child reflects
the nature of this is dark
but the mirrors are weightless

when the cold landscape melts
contradictory values may return
as the body grows and grows
into the art of being itself
some forces remain and not others
but who knows where to fall
I see the light beneath my feet
and my body is weightless

opening . . .

opening the gate
for one another
your image
leaves its bed
and walks

this silvery light
outside its cage
leans forward
like a river's
precious banks

toward still water
you see your face
as part of a face
the sign
which remains

a hundred miles up
a world
is constructed
and then burns
you wear my coat

and I'll take yours
we'll face the brightness
together
opening the gate
for one another

the small girl . . .

the small girl drives the police car
                        towards a cloud
it is absurd
                like every cry from every street
the siren astonishes us, too
                        what disasters of the night!
THE MILKMAN HAS CUT OFF HIS HAND

method is no distraction
                    it is the simple image of the road
and its attendant spirits
                            the street accident
for instance
                is one among many noises
the cloud turns into a mountain

her arm is covered by snow
                    we were completely at home
'has she asked us to stay'
                        and oh so many jokes
were silent and Joe dear
                Joe pretended to sleep
and so the century wore on

The secret is . . .

The secret is in the hands of . . . . . . good grief!
when you think of the evidence against us
an embrace of real things as if without colour
whilst Mankind riding the starry firmament
the sickly light of the hairbrush is pronounced
thus and thus I love you and you turn me on
third party. His eye wanders from line to line
setting at a distance all that was said
ditto the sea of faces while

it is 4 o'clock and 77 degrees
sweet smoke and silver print
of the afternoon shining
as right as rain
in a clear, calm voice
she began the story of her life
every store has a name
the cup darkens its saucer
similar noises are breathed
by the pool and its pageant
of wrongs for crying out loud
there are tears in her ears
over you
it's a great feeling

suzanne by camouflaging her language has run
into the sunshine with a key to these structures
as green as grass that our playmates
are naturally refreshed after the vast heat
has approached thus the smell of mortal frames
like a river of various import. What rage is this
dear heart the cat has disappeared but not
the grin now the flares go up and the butler stands
amazed and troubled within himself

there is a surface of things which seems
to move but does not o death where is thy sting
the flame will leap up and so die to stare
at one life dear god the very houses seem
(move over stupid this is toytown) o grave where is
thy victory the drowning man watches
tiny gilded butterflies whilst Mr. Plod the policeman
goes on his rounds again, dreaming
of Jeannie with the light brown hair.

a true resemblance . . .

a true resemblance
portraits in flowers
in the general sphere

an actual world
the retrospective
musical evening

ends in tears,
its proper self,
between his legs

no one got out alive
the plants grew
into specific forms

absolute indifference
enters the mess
like a fuck

"we love each other
but the time-bomb
broke the pianoforte"

you do the best . . .

you do the best things in silence
moving around in the morning as if you were still
moving your arms in your sleep

the light greets you like a simile
which compares your silence with its own
an image of childhood

taken from the pantomime version of *Swan Lake*
your youth will be open and free
you will write out poems in long hand

in recognition of your true feelings
among the dwarf trees which shelter you :
this is the street where I was born

and here are the people, in see-saw motion,
change turning to strangeness
my life is their life in miniature

each one is getting dispersed
moving away from the centre, which never existed,
into a region of greenish light

like creatures from Wells's *The Time Machine*
our happiness defined by our labour
human voices stirred by the distance

Foolish Tears

People today are always having problems and difficulties within their own personal families. Foolish Tears is somewhat about family problems, but not problems just difficulties.

I enjoyed writing Foolish Tears and thought that David Watts was my favourite character in the poem. He seemed like a type of guy who was shy, but still wanted to marry this certain girl. He went to his friend and was going to ask for help but his friend was married to the person David wanted to marry.

I liked David because he is somewhat the same as I. A person who is shy even to talk to a girl but still is "madly" in love with her. David was a quiet somewhat subdued person. When David's friend found out David liked his wife he didn't seem to mind; he even tried to get David and his wife together. David was embarrassed for a while but not for long.

Foolish Tears is a confusing poem and it was hard to keep the people straight. Who was married to whom and so forth. Even though it was confusing I still enjoyed writing it, and I think I am a good writer.

194 words including title.

Deliver me . . .

Deliver me out of this and
for the first time you look up
        as a stranger, awake

from all possible harm. You are
nowhere on earth now, I know
        this as a risk,

as you turn back to sleep. Deliver
me out of this place, quietly,
        as you breathe,
    my rise and my fall.

Something . . .

Something that has been somewhere far away,
is still remote but we no longer desire it,
like this boy in the field, or the outer family
of stars, so we dream of each other. Fair
rocks, goodly rivers, sweet woods, and yon grassy
mountains, where shall I find peace?
The restaurant is bathed in tears, not tears,
but quiet days, O do not die, sweet boy,
they are the music of the spheres. Here,
I am holding them toward you. Your heart will melt.

Homecoming

The person or persons unknown
Have stolen the rhyme
They have left specimens
Of their handwriting

Strelitzias also bloom
Under the varnish
Which haunts us
Like a missing button

Imagine,
The boy walks his pooch
In an unearthly silence
Waiting for a sign

The first day was quiet
Your body rose among
Tiny objects, and became
A surface that shone

I who am of sound mind
And body do hereby
Wake up for no reason,
Whose are these words

Which will free us
A red biplane writes A
Across a cloud and ah
Touches the ground.

To persist in . . .

> To persist in the situation to be tired of
> "everything must have a point, Tom"
> but these things are beyond mere words.
> Static Electricity is my only friend
> blue may fall apart but life
>
> goes on. Won't somebody tell me,
> where have all the good times gone? Flash.
> Any form is the perspective of another form . . .
> I love you so much I could eat you.
> Yessir we do believe certain, uh, things.

You sing . . .

You sing at extreme moments
watching your life until it is still

winding and unwinding the mystery,
when did everything change

in the second degree of sleep
the aircraft signal each other

your face is turned to the wall
and we have brought sounds toward you

you see the day from this house
like the smooth face of the blast

will you go through your life alone
to unravel the stain which falls

in sequence, my aviator companion
these volumes speak of your last gasp.

A prose poem

Underwear or toilet accessories : this was an age-long dilemma, worrying Arthur almost to extinction. All those sunny days, when Arthur felt sick with gratification. "But sex isn't the same thing as love," he used to say and the police vans went whizzing by. What a mountain of anguish arises from that small word, life!

Dark night, its dreadful margins, castrates these elves. Arthur sits reading the small print of the wallpaper. Suburban rackets vanish in a miasma of wires, clues grind to a climax. Arthur sleeps peacefully below the harvest moon.

Bold words, sire! the garage owner spits into his pump. Th'art strong and sure! All over the world small men climbed trees. The ink descends, flags scatter many ways. Is this a dream perchance to. Arise Arthur. Great morning has popped the question. Oh do not ask what is it.

The weak chimneys of Arthur's heart blew and reblew. He recollected several childhood experiences, the blonde building site. Arthur smiles at his phylogenesis. The demolition was turquoise. His future valise arrives.

Rocks and footfalls. Marcel Proust! Steam and our present selves! Arthur, come home! These calls, it is the right kind of freedom.

to walk . . .

to walk away
and to stand
your hands, the sands
but the question
is asking itself

howinsasmuchas
of words and cries
a vast effigy
is moving away
to a vast effigy

of the embrace
of real things
your desire
for those words
the closed window

and then . . .

and then they were freed . . .
and light touch of economy
will dilate these curtains
which are apparent singing
of the whole man who strides
over his own vision of land
and peels the orange until
he feels the pang of injustice
afflicting the rain that now
leaves me cold and unsettled
as the running man in sight
of the stairs where the child
considers his past and is
restless once more asking
of small creatures do you exist
as I do but they fall in
silence expecting the night
as I pass my hand over my face
and it is sufficient for the
moment to pass into a question
of gain and of loss for the
story is now a fragment that I
may walk in new freedom

the hermaphrodite . . .

the hermaphrodite suffers a change : now he is alone
and the surface is wonderful,   he sits in the silence
of trains, he just reads old magazines

you have reached the desert station, and your perfect
friends are out of place; their ironies make your
heart thump

on looking into the world, your eyes got bloodshot;
the poet wears violet shades, he is dreaming of things
to come. Alas his art is dead.

the slight track of events, the last cigarette;
listen! we can obtain the world! the grief-stricken
multitudes

ah where have you gone, these words are pillars of salt

the poet sucks off the circus-boy, he alone knows his
true value; sexual practices decorate the wonderful smile
of his father. The poet dreams of bare-back riding.

there is semen on his chin : yes he is alive, too; also
there is love without end.

The first axiom . . .

The first axiom of this proposition is that the firppppppppppppp

thc the the the the the the the the the

spanish fly, my own true

tttttttttooopppppppppppoopopopopopopopopo

by the banks of the Iffey I

ooooooooooooooooooooooooooh

and so to bed, and so to bed, and so to bed, and so to bed

ouch

whatisthislifeiffullofcarewehavenotimeto

the supreme penalty

is   is   is   is   is

I took . . .

I took the children onto the plain, and it has begun to snow. There are some curtains and it is quiet, I think. We are building small huts out of the fresh snow and now we are sleeping in them. The orphans have noticed that a large moon is rising in the right-hand corner, and the clay melted away from our arms. The centre of the day is too bright, or too small, to be seen. I shook the glass sphere which held the miniature landscape, and watched the ash fall down through it.

A love poem

How do you wring your hands
so that to go up in smoke . . .
the note divides like a note

how have you bin? Pretty good
so far at least. Anyways so
little thinks't thou poor flower

despite this sorrow as fresh
and ever-renewed as a tear
you are small and sexy I dig you

this continuing disharmony
makes for harmony, my dear,
I mean it sincerely ouch

during the song of the night
as it is broadcast to you
the complete sphere of wonder

in the boredom of a scream :
the infant twinkles his eye,
blue murder, stairway to heaven.

The great Sun . . .

The great Sun wastes its energy upon small objects
and catches me in the art of being myself,
I can relax a bit while the light rushes by
past the houses and the people in the houses.
A general English melancholy settles down
as the birds dip their beaks into the earth —
the flies have had a long life this year as well
but a hand may pass across the Sun
and I will not understand these things.

The light falls across various emotions
until they become the simple idea of myself
at the foot of a crag, for instance, enduring
                    the fear of death
as my breath streaks across the firmament.
Actually, the light has vanished through a gap
                    in these personifications,
the sky is changing into a map of the new order
and I am left behind in the march of events.

The little tune . . .

           The little tune
                just about makes it,
           across the water
                    the shadows steal away
leaving the wreck behind.

           How amazing
        to leave the past
        as you would leave a ship,
                coming out dazed
the lights on your face.

Across the water
        it gets so dark
     we can go no further,
             now the small craft
are being carried away.

           See you soon! I love you!
When this river is no longer
                a metaphor for time
        I will still love you!
Oh shine the torches,

Captain, we drift.
     I left my notes
upon the wreck,
        and the tuneless sky
is rushing above us.

We loved . . .

We loved not yet nor quite
21 — 24 E is the girl who would not
wake up W is pure joy,
it's modern, it's sexy, it's a work of
genius, sing the same song
brother this is the happiest day of.
Would you believe
as dreams eat love like sweets.

watching the process . . .

                watching the process
                      for signs of wear
        I saw words on the page
                        continually breaking in
            unenviable rhythm

            my mouth is working
    but where is the food
                    the sky is falling
        the sky is falling
           but where is the ground

      'each thing in its own season'
    and such sophistication
        is fine in green times
                but in this place
    where no one has a home?

            the failure is
          'to still the beating heart'
             the same feelings
                come back
                and in the same words

        the ideas are sufficient
            for the space provided
    that each line is clear :
            the roof has fallen

        and the light is coming in

to distinguish
between

during the meal
little was said
as the fork rose
and fell, adieu
things that are
I bleed continually
for you it is
a twice-told tale

today and everyday
the home calleth

yr decision is
for ever and ever
a quick exit
from the green whore
alas my love
you have done, crabby
the day which flies
toward you
but this mood
will never last

when suddenly
out of the blue

the meat
walking on grass
such people pass
like flames
into each other
they laugh
in unison,
in a brown study
let me count the ways
of white, crimson
and rose carmethian

It was no longer . . .

It was no longer warm, the sun grew larger as if someone
had entered the room. Everything is being shaken into
a half-awakened life.

We brace ourselves against what we deserve, like the wind
which brings snow. I think I am smiling, therefore
I am smiling. Everything flies to its place

which is invisible. The child has finished his story
and he, too, is alone. The lamps are still burning
although we left the place long ago, swamped in tears.

But the moon is out tonight, and the prince will turn
into a pauper, who is his double, everything
is touching everything else. Just look how the snow.

all these . . .

all these particles of knowledge
are a stick which I carry in my hand
pulled out of the vast emptiness
of a day at the sea

I looked up into the branches
and I saw nothing
except the wind
and its persistent insect

the dunes incline towards me
and the noisome truth
is the knowledge
that you will have to leave this place

the branch floating down
haunted by itself
as a body
having to change what it loves

love falls . . .

love falls
       as brightness
moving from each to each

       'sleep forever'
     the boy said
           who had no job

and no chance of getting one
       turning on the stair
each with his own grace

     one with too much passion
one had a nice face
           you can see things

in whatever order
           you want
     and then, forgetting

       this snow drifts
                 over my feet
           a complete light

       leaving me afraid
     I will not turn back
           along the empty ways

there are so many emotions to get through
that I dream continually of slipping backwards
while the day spins ahead of me like a kite
although its string leads precisely nowhere

or perhaps it leads back to my hand
as it makes ineffectual gestures against the sky
as though sketching out some great plot
which will encircle all of our feelings

I suppose this is a definition of madness
being detached from life and yet needing it
so that the smallest resentments can kill
and the poet drifts morosely into the evening

which never satisfies him, while sober,
but which he may choose to write 'about'.
So everything proceeds by misdirection
while all around us the laundry piles up

and there is nothing to be done
except to go on to the next task, and then the next,
receiving brickbats and letters of thanks
as if they were the most natural thing in the world

since it must be assumed that someone is watching
otherwise my behaviour would be extreme
and there would be no more time for my writing —
but then these poems will be a complete statement!

the empty telephone . . .

the empty telephone of yore
and my sole self to fall asleep
as a continuation perchance to
talk with bated breath to here I
am whose life has thus gone on

Acknowledgments

Certain of these poems have appeared in
Ouch (The Curiously Strong Press, 1971)
London Lickpenny (Ferry Press, 1973)
Country Life (Ferry Press, 1978).